Dedicant's Handbook
to
Coven Life

House of Witchcraft

Taren S

DEDICATION

To all the Witches who are finding their way home. We were waiting for you and have kept the sacred fires lit.

Sometimes, we put our secrets in the open, so no one will see them.

That which seen will be unseen to the mundane. That which is like energy will easily be found.

CONTENTS

Introduction

Welcome Home
The Cottage door is always open to the Witchery folks that find their way there. Each lifetime we return to the sacred fires our spirits know. We all have chosen to travel the road less taken. Somehow, knowing it is the right one.

Now know, you are not alone. This is the first step in a magickal journey of self-discovery.

Keep this book safe, and use the wisdom and knowledge in any way you see fit.

Living on the Crossroads
Once a Witch, always a Witch. It matters not the family, or the land born on but the spirit. If you feel Witchy, then you are Witchy.

To be a Witch is not to read a special book or stand in a special circle in a special way. It is to 'feel' that special inside of you. Words have a hard time conveying this. How do you explain that you just 'feel it'? No one told you. It wasn't given a name.

When you stand in a grove of trees and the wind blows through you, breathing its energies into you. You are a part of it, the wind; and it is a part of you. It is in your spirit. Or when you stand under the moonlight and the rays fill your insides with an un-named power.

A power that tells you that you are not alone. That you are part of something... greater. Something to be respected and honored. Something that holds the secrets of the universe, if you are willing to listen.

Magickal Puberty

Many of the Witchery folks have a common story. We all went through a stage or time when we came to the conclusion that we just might be a Witch. We experienced magickal puberty.

No one told us this, many of us had never even been near a Witch before. From somewhere deep inside our spirit it came; we are magickal and we are Witchy.

Sometime between 11-14 years old is when most of us came into the realization that we weren't quite like the other kids. And our search for finding out where we belong began.

Stepping into magickal space for the first time was like coming home for most of us. Somehow, you had the sense that you had been here before. Finally, a world where it all made sense. A place of like-minded folks welcoming you home to where you truly belong.

This is your magickal, mystical, Divine journey to take.

I will love myself.
I will forgive myself.
I will be true to myself.
How I treat myself is the standard for how others will treat me.
Author unknown

1 OPENING THE DOOR

You must start at the beginning and
create from what is present.
And so begins this journey.......

Becoming A Dedicant
Come to a min. of 3 events at the Cottage.
Read and agree to follow the House of Witchcraft membership rules.
Read the "Dedicant's Handbook to Coven Life" (the book you are reading right now.).
Schedule a private meeting to discuss your Dedication/Rite of Beginning (if you desire one) and begin your Year and a Day journey. This is NOT the Initiation into our Tradition.

The Dedication Rite is simply a self-acknowledgment to being Witchy, to being magickal, and dedicating your life to this journey.

Some Witches want a Dedication to Divinity (Goddess for some) when they start their magickal journey. This is a Rite of Self, that is between you and Divinity and no one else. For some new Witches, this is a very important Rite, whether done privately or with the coven.

Dedicate is a two-meaning word in the Witchy world. Many Witches may dedicate themselves to a certain Deity or magickal path. They may reference themselves as a devotee to a Deity.

A Dedicate may also mean the year and a day time period before joining a coven. We have both types of Dedications and periodically confuse folks when discussing either.

Ask questions and remember what you "think" a word means may not be the same for the person speaking.

Dedications are traditionally done during the full moon or when the time feels right for the Witch. Which moon (new, full, dark), which month, or season to do your dedication is each Witch's personal choice. For some there is a special time of the year that they want to start their journey, while for others it is the next full moon.

Once a date has been set, all members are invited to attend the ritual. The Dedication commitment is to Divinity and to yourself. We take no vows to earthly creatures for spiritual/magickal matters.

The only vow you will ever take to the Tradition is silence. To protect those who stand in sacred space with you by never speaking their mundane names.

It is during this year and a day time period (or longer if you choose) you must state aloud three (3) times your intent to join the coven. This is your decision, and no one will ask, inquire, or cajole you about this. Joining any Tradition is a serious undertaking, and we expect deep self-consideration before taking this step.

The Rite of Initiation into the House of Witchcraft Tradition is done after standing in magickal space with the coven for a year and a day, with all Initiated Witches to the coven in agreement of said membership. The only vow we ask anyone to take is to protect the names of the other Witches we stand shoulder to shoulder with.

First Year and a Day

By making the commitment to yourself and Divinity to stand under every full moon for a year and a day to open yourself up to the magick of universe; your life will change. You will be different. The journey is personal, and growth comes in unexpected ways.

Each Witch's path is unique, special and very personal. For some, this first year and a day is spent in personal exploration in a Traditional coven environment, while others will want to start working on First Degree commitments and knowledge. With counsel, you will decide which is best for you. The right way is your way.

During this time, all Dedicants should be using the information in this book to help/aid them in their journey. Each Full Moon answer the Witchy prompts at the end of the chapters throughout this book. DO NOT sit down and try to answer the questions all at once.

This is a journey, embrace the entire experience and with each new pebble turned, you will find the next step. Short cuts are just cutting you out of the journey.

Dedicates Are Expected:

To have their physical/mundane lives at a healthy stage to explore/experience their spiritual/magickal selves.

To attend 75% of all activities/events at the Cottage during the calendar year.

To donate funds that you can afford to help with supporting the Cottage.

To help and assist with activities/events at the Cottage.

3

To attend/support activities/events in the Pagan community at-large whenever possible.

◆◆◆

To have a blessed book/journal/bos.

◆◆◆

To have a handwritten copy of "The Witch's Way" in personal journal/bos.

◆◆◆

To start working on form(s) of divination that interest you.

◆◆◆

To learn different ways to create sacred space (cast circle).

◆◆◆

To cast/create a minimum of two (2) circles for Cottage events (full, new, dark moons) during your year and a day journey.

◆◆◆

To develop a list of 15 favorite herbs or more and uses. Use them.

◆◆◆

To ask the Universe for aid in acquiring magickal tools needed (or wanted).

◆◆◆

To have a special robe, cloak, or garment for magickal use only. Wear it.

◆◆◆

To deepen relationship with Divinity by setting up a personal altar, daily mantras, and any other way you personally relate to. Put Divinity in your Daily Life.

◆◆◆

To actively seek to be in a "state of service" to yourself and others.

◆◆◆

To keep a record of each full moon experience during your year and a day journey in your bos. Time, date, aspects, workings done, how you felt, predictions, things learned, thoughts written each time you stand in sacred space. NEVER write down another's mundane name, only use their magickal name or your personal code.

To ask aloud three (3) times in sacred space to be initiated into the House of Witchcraft lineage after standing under 13 moons or longer with the group.

Books to Read
The following books are required (strongly recommended) reading for all Cottage Witches.

"Natural Magic" by Doreen Valiente

"America Bewitched- The story of Witchcraft after Salem", by Owen Davies

"Natural Witchery'" by Ellen Dugan

"Dedicant's Handbook To Covenlife", by Taren S

"Way of the Magus", by Michael Howard

Optional Bonus Scholarly Reading**

"Introduction to Pagan Studies", by Barbara Jane Davy

"Triumph of the Moon", by Ronald Hutton

A year and a day is mother nature's lesson time. When we experience this cycle, we become a part of it. Each new season brings us new lessons and knowledge- let your magick reflect that. Spring is the time of awakenings, beginnings. Fall brings us harvest and change. Winter is when the earth sleeps and things move slowly. Summer is growing and full of warmth.

Initiates
After you have completed your year and a day, completed the

Dedicant's requirements and asked three (3) times for initiation/membership into the Tradition, a vote by members will take place. A 100% agreement by coven of Dedicant becoming an Initiated member to the Tradition is required.

A time/place for initiation ritual will be discussed privately with individual.

Membership of Witches' Cottage

Membership is open to all folks over 18 yrs old.

The group is egalitarian in all matters. 75% approval needed of active members and those who happen to be present in most matters regarding the coven. Everyone has a vote and gets a say in matters.

Substance abuse of any kind will not be tolerated. You will be asked to leave and not return.

All folks in physical as well as astral realms will be treated with respect.

No profanity in the Cottage. Please just try.

Active member is anyone who has attended 75% of events/activities available to them and is Dedicated.

Clothing of some type is required for all activities/events at the Cottage.

Any physical threats or aggression towards anyone will involve law enforcement. (they have just lost their minds)

All members will strive to be a productive member of society, both magickal and mundane.

All members will strive to live their life's in accordance with The Witch's Way.

All members are open to join any other magickal or mundane organization they see fit to do so.

All members may terminate membership at anytime by simply stating so. Once this is done, a 100% approval vote from all active members is needed to return.

Membership rules may be changed/altered/deleted/added at Imbolc with 75% approval.

Done Got Up and Left Clause
If any member of the Witches' Cottage is not in contact with the group for 5 months or longer, we will consider you "done got up and left" and remove you from membership. Membership may be re-instated anytime with a 100% approval vote from all active members.

Witches' Cottage Rule
No green bean casseroles for potluck

Offices Within the Witches' Cottage
Offices/duties will be held on an annual basis from Imbolc to Imbolc. Offices/duties can be added or deleted during Imbolc for the coming year when there is a need. 75% approval needed to make change. Members may only hold one office during the calendar year.

Current Offices are:
Group chat office is responsible for adding/deleting names in group chat.
Bonfire duties is responsible for safety around the fire.
Greetings Committee is responsible for welcoming/helping/assisting new folks at the Cottage.
Holder of the Wine cork opener is responsible for knowing at all times where the gadget is and can in a timely matter access such said item for immediate use.

Degrees
After your year and a day journey standing under the moons with the Witches' Cottage you may ask to join the coven. This is done by stating aloud your intent in sacred space three (3) times with at least 2 active members present.
The coven will vote upon final membership after hearing third statement of intent and notify the Dedicate in a timely fashion. In this matter, a 100% vote in favor of dedicate is required.

House of Witchcraft uses a traditional 3 Degree System for a way of gauging knowledge and experience. There is no minimum or maximum time allotted for each season.

You will know when the time is right to move forward in the system if that is what you desire. Becoming a 3rd Degree does not automatically make someone a High Priest type. That honor is given by the person's peers/hive-off. Folks will know you are a High Priestess before you do.

◆◆◆

At First Degree, we give you back to yourself.

◆◆◆

At Second Degree, we give you back to the community.

◆◆◆

Third Degree, we give you back to the Gods.

◆◆◆

(First Degree folks work on their personal knowledge base. Second Degree folks expand to understanding more about the workings of the magickal world at large. Third Degree folks stand center a sacred or magickal space and pick up garbage after everyone has left.)

The circle is cast, we are between worlds, in the space that knows no time.
Be brave and part the veil, for now is your time to walk through.

Mother Goddess hear my prayer,
hold me in thy loving care.
Father God watch over me to
guide me and all that I can do.
Make us safe within the night,
and bless us with the mornings light.
So shall it be.

Lady Abigail

When I do magick I feel

_____

_____

_____

_____

My energy flows when

_____

_____

_____

_____

The circle of life means to me that

_____

_____

_____

_____

Standing in magickal space makes me feel

_____

_____

_____

_____

When I look in the mirror, I see

_____

_____

_____

_____

My mundane protection is

_____

_____

_____

_____

My magickal protection is

_____

_____

_____

_____

My strength is

_____

_____

_____

_____

My weakness is

_____

_____

_____

_____

I seek

_____

_____

_____

_____

I am a Witch because

_____

_____

_____

_____

Being supported by other Witches means

_____

_____

_____

_____

I feel really good when

_____

_____

_____

_____

10 Blessings in my life right now are:

1.

2.

3.

4.

5.

6.

7.

8.

9.

10.

I am magickal because

_____

_____

_____

_____

My priorities are

_____

_____

_____

_____

In 10 years from now, I will have

_____

_____

_____

_____

Divinity whispered in my ear and said

_____

_____

2 WITCHES & OUR HISTORY

House of Witchcraft is...
We are a Crossroads Witchcraft Tradition with roots starting in the mountains of Virginia by a talented folk magick healer at the turn of the 19th century (approx. 1904).
Each generation has added more depth and magick to our lineage. Today we stand as testament to those folks who taught us that "Divinity is within" and gave us a solid foundation to benefit from all the magick in the crossroads.

Taren S is 5th generation in the House. She was initiated in 1987 in North Carolina and began her journey to standing center in sacred space. In 1992 she founded the Circle in the Willows coven, a hive-off of the Tradition in the Lowcountry of South Carolina. CiW's season lasted almost 14 years and 4 covens are currently direct hive-off's from it.

The Witches' Cottage is the latest coven to form from this part of the lineage. Oct. '18 Full moon was the first circle cast for the Witches' Cottage coven, calling on like-minded Witches in the region to come a dance magick around the bonfire. The Cottage's magick comes from the Witches who stand in the sacred circle together here in Southern California.

Each coven in the Tradition is self-governing with a High Priest or leader type chosen by that group. While the covens are considered "sisters", they in no way co-ordinate or operate a hierarchy. Each coven is its' own distinct flavor of magick of those folks, and the dirt they stand upon.

State of Service
To receive blessings, we must first be able to give them.

Within our Tradition, each coven/group will have an active "state of service" that they give to the magickal and/or mundane community. A state of service is defined as being a part of your community in a positive matter, however each coven/member decides that action. Helping at community shelters, food drives, donating clothing, leading public Sabbats are just a few of the ways our members do this.

The Witches' Cottage's state of service is an open teaching circle welcoming Witches returning home. We will aid, assist and help fellow magickal folks on their journeys whether they decide to dance with us or go elsewhere. Our goal is to be a door that opens the seeker to the magickal world that awaits them.

We are an open teaching tradition that encourages hive offs and journeys of self-discoveries. Legacy is our main focus; not what we are given but what we leave behind.

Legacy is:
-teachings   -wisdom   -humor
-traditions   -honesty -memories
-loyalty   -inspiration

Our magick is the magick of our ancestors. We do not strive to re-create their moments, but to use them to inspire us to have our moments. Just as they too looked to those before them, so do we. This is our magickal circle-it's a reflection of the past, while looking to the future, and standing in the present moment.

Crossroads Witchcraft

Crossroads Witchcraft is the blending of folk magick from many cultures and the ancient European, African and South American magickal systems. Southeastern part of America is where we find the oldest roots of this blending. It is called Hoodoo by many folks.

Hoodoo has strong regional roots determined by the folks that were either brought (slaves) or immigrated to that particular area and the Natives already there. The Hoodoo of South Carolina is strongly influenced by the Haitians, Irish, Sierra Leone region of Africa, Scotch-Irish, and the Native tribes in that region.

The Hoodoo of New Orleans is more of a blend of Caribbean, French, and the Native folks there. The Appalachian Mountains folks have deep roots in the British Isles magick and the Pow-wow magick of the Pennsylvania Dutch is traced to Germanic influences.

While each region seems to be distinctly separate, what unites all Hoodoo folks is three (3) principles: connecting to Divinity, connecting to Spiritual realms and connecting to the land we stand on.

Hoodoo Witchery

Celebrating the Dirt we stand on.

The House of Witchcraft is an American Crossroads Witchcraft tradition celebrating the balance of dark and light. The house embraces diversity and the global magickal crossroads that lead us to the deep spiritual paths that Divinity has to offer.

Through the land we stand on, connections with Ancestral realms, and a personal relationship with Divinity, we embrace all the magick that the world has to offer. From Africa to Ireland, we are a land of many paths that now walk hand in hand. We respect differences while celebrating unity.

We are Witchery

Witchery- noun, verb, adjective. The creating of magick within ourselves by embracing the land we stand upon, giving honor to Ancestral realms, and developing a relationship with Divinity.

Our Magick

Witchery folks develop a highly personalized system of magick that works for them. Your own personal recipe book, just like Grandma had.

Moon Sisters/Brothers

Once the group has stood in a sacred space under a full moon for a year and a day, there is a bond created among the folks that are a part of it. These folks become moon sisters and moon brothers to each other. The group becomes a magickal family. These are bonds that last a lifetime and beyond.

I will love myself.
I will forgive myself.
I will be true to myself.
How I treat myself is the standard for how others will treat me.

Read this, over & over.

Why Witches Wear Black

Witches traditionally wear black because black absorbs all the colors of the visible spectrum and reflects none of them to the eyes. It draws in all natural energies, enhances the strength of one's personal power, and connection to nature.

The Color Purple

Traditionally, Witches like the color purple, and often times paint the front door of their home the deep warm hues of the color.

"A purple door is the door to open mindedness, intuition, awakening of the sub consciousness. It often represents the homestead of a witch, or practitioner of magick, who understands higher levels of consciousness, and how to live a prosperous life beyond monetary gain." The White Witch Path

Purple Flowers

Keep purple flowers by a window that faced the moonlight to draw in healing energies to the 3rd eye and help open the window to the sub consciousness.

You are a wise, wondrous, and powerful Spirit.
You radiate beauty and light.
Embrace your beautiful soul and know that you are perfect, just the way you are.
Have faith in yourself, for you have the ability to manifest great things in your life, if you just put your heart and mind to it.
Live your life with intention, a compassionate heart, and a great purpose.

I find magick in

_____

_____

_____

_____

A magickal mystery is

_____

_____

_____

_____

I want other Witches to know about me

_____

_____

_____

I feel safe when

_____

_____

_____

A loving heart is

_____

_____

_____

A vow I take is

_____

_____

_____

When I have been wronged, I

_____

_____

_____

I deserve to be

_____

_____

_____

_____

Dancing with Witches is

_____

_____

_____

I dream most often about

_____

_____

_____

Faith is

_____

_____

_____

Other people's opinions are

_____

_____

_____

A year & a Day means to me

_____

_____

_____

_____

3 FINDING YOUR MAGICKAL SELF

Upping Your Magickal Vibrations
The first step to doing magick is understanding you are the magick.
Belief of self is the foundation in any magickal undertaking. When
you truly believe you are magickal is when the magick happens. To
start embracing the magick that is already within you, spend a moon
cycle or two or three tuning into yourself. Upping your magickal
vibrations so to speak.

There is a difference in doing a magickal working and just following
instructions. It is all about your headspace and the energy you have
created around you. Here is the working for helping you to embrace
the magick that is within.

Spend time really thinking about the answers to the questions before
writing them down. Although some of the questions may seem
mundane, they help you to understand you just a little more. So,
when you stand before a Deity (Divinity), you can truly say "I know
who I am." And that is the beginning of a very powerful magickal
working.

Step 1
Start under a full moon. Create sacred space/cast a circle. Prepare a
small altar and say a prayer to Divinity. Light a candle, or not. This

is the beginning of your magickal working/spell/incantation journey. Add a little personal flair!

Ask for wisdom and clarity to guide you on this magickal awakening. Ask for protection and understanding. Use your words and write them in your journal.

Don't forget to date the entry. This is a moment in time you will look back upon. Close your circle/space.

Now the work begins:

Spend the moon cycle (til the next full moon) working on the following:

Ask yourself the following questions and write the answers in your journal or here

◆◆◆

When do you feel most magickal?

_____

_____

_____

_____

What does luxury mean to you?

_____

_____

_____

_____

What are 5 things you love about yourself without a doubt?

_____

_____

_____

_____

What is the one message you want to share with the world?

_____

_____

_____

_____

What is your favorite time of the day? What makes it so special?

_____

_____

_____

What is the worst thing that could happen if you said no?

_____

_____

_____

What is the one place near your home that you have always wanted to visit?

_____

_____

_____

What are some gifts-tangible or not-that you need to give to yourself?

_____

_____

_____

In this moment, what are 5 things you know to be absolutely true?

_____

_____

_____

Instead of a to-do list, make a tah-dah list celebrating all the good things you have done lately.

_____

_____

_____

_____

CAYA
Come As You Are

Find your path in Self.
Strengthen it in Family.
Live it through the Community.

The Golden Rule of Magick
To Know - To Will - To Dare - To Keep Silent

To Know
Knowledge is the cornerstone to all activities in the magickal realms.
Don't just rely on one source. Instead gather as much information as
you can on the subject. Even contrary or conflicting views will give
you more insight. Always look to discover new ideas, not confirm
beliefs held. Keep open to new ideas, ways, methods, and you will
always be growing.

To Dare
Action with knowledge is to dare. What stops most folks is belief of
self. 3 words that many spend a lifetime never achieving. You must
dare to put the knowledge you have learned to use.

To Will
To have no doubt. Never speaking of "if it works" only "when it
works". When the word "if" is used it creates a place for doubt to
grow and ultimately failure is the result. When we do a

spell/working we always want to speak as if it has already successfully happened.

To Keep Silent

When we let others know what we are doing, we are giving them an opportunity to influence our work. Maybe that is a good thing, or just maybe that is a bad thing. Why take the chance?

How to Do Magick

There is no right way, one way, best way, secret way, real way, or oldest way. There is only your way. The right way is your way. The right way is what feels right.

"I use a personalized system of magick that works for me."

The Myth of "The Way"

Worst myth ever!! Blame it on the first set of instructions for the mess. The first person who said, "this is the way you do magick" was only giving his opinion. Because if he was the first, who the hell told him? Ahh, like maybe he was doing what felt right?

What we think,
we create.
What we feel,
we attract.
What we imagine,
we become.

My sacred temple is

_____

_____

_____

_____

Solitude verus being alone means to me

_____

_____

_____

To command a space, you must

_____

_____

_____

My truth is

_____

_____

_____

I want a relationship with Divinity because

_____

_____

_____

Other people's magick is

_____

_____

_____

_____

A Peer is

_____

_____

_____

In the Spirit Realm, I connect

_____

_____

_____

When I do a good job, I feel

_____

_____

_____

My magick is

_____

_____

_____

Being in the moment means to me

_____

_____

_____

Wealth means

_____

_____

4 CREATE YOUR MAGICKAL LIFE

If you want to create a beautiful magickal life, then you must plant a seed of beauty within yourself. Write a daily uplifting note to yourself for the next 30 days in your journal.

"A beautiful day begins with a beautiful mindset. Every day you wake up, think about what a privilege it is to simply be alive and healthy. Stop focusing on the negatives and everything that could go wrong and start thinking about what could go right. Be thankful for nights that turned into mornings, friends who became family and past dreams and goals that turned into realities. Use this mindset of positivity to fuel an even brighter today and tomorrow." John Geiger

Create a Personal Mantra
Create a short mantra you recite to yourself when needed. Post it on your bathroom mirror. Say it daily.

Examples:
"I am a most awesome magickal Witch."
"I am the Goddess."
"The Goddess is within me."
"I am astral born and the Goddess is my soul."
"I am Divine, and Divinity is within me."

Now you have a solid foundation of Self; where the magick is. Time to open the grimoire for more possibilities and growth. Stand under each Full Moon and strive to be in the moment, and the universe will aid you in your magickal undertakings.

Every Moon Cycle
Cast a magickal circle, make moon blessed water, do prosperity spells/workings, send healing energies to those in need, develop a relationship with Divinity, dance and make merry around a bonfire.

Magickal Life Wisdom
Don't be afraid of mistakes.
Embrace-Learn-Change-Grow

Own your shit, or as polite folk would say "take responsibility for your actions". I have lost count of how many times I have said "that was my idea that didn't work." I now know another way not to do something. And really, is that a bad thing?

Experience is often how not to do something. Good judgement is not to do it again.

Be in the Moment!
Look to mother nature, the universe, what is happening in the present moment around you to dictate the type of circle you cast for that moon cycle.

Each moon has unique energies, tune into that and use it. Never be afraid to throw out what you had planned and do something entirely different when standing in the present moment.

What we sometimes planned to do while sitting in the cottage, and what we really did in our sacred space are often two very different things. And even though we didn't "use" what we had planned, we still took that energy into circle with us. Nothing is ever wasted.

Importance of Ritual Bath/Shower

The importance of getting in the right head space BEFORE entering sacred or magickal space - Why we take ritual bath/showers. This is probably the most common error among the new magickal folk. In our time saving world, and now-now attitudes, we try to condense and concise things.

Often, we skip a step or combine two tasks into one. You can do many things with tweaking workings (spells), but you can't do shortcuts when it comes to activating the magick that is within you. You need to change your vibrations and open yourself up to magickal possibilities.

That is the simplest explanation to be given without getting into human Psychology, Occult theory, and a tad bit of Quantum physics. Really, everything is connected, and science can prove it.

The easiest way to do this is with the use of water and a magickal ritual soap. The use of water in sacred or magickal ways has been traced into pre-history. The herbs and essential oils in the soap have their own vibrations that will help to awaken all your senses. And you will feel the difference.

There is no one super magickal soap recipe that works for everybody. Yes, I know you're disappointed. You were hoping we were going to give you a recipe for your soap. But I ask you, how can we do that? How can we know what is right for you? The only person that knows that is you. A little research and you will find herbs and essential oils that resonate with you.

Start with just a few drops of essential oils and to make sure any herbs that you use are organically sourced and contain no chemicals. Keep it simple with creating a recipe that may only have 2 or 3 ingredients. There is no need to make a 15 item concoction. Save that for later.

Magickal soap blends will change season to season. Also, many Witches have different soap blends for different workings.

Basic Magickal Soap Recipe

Goat's milk soap base (can be bought at local craft store & just need a microwave oven) few drops of lavender & cucumber oil, dried lemon or mint leaves, crushed apricot seed (excellent exfoliant-scrubby stuff). Mix and pour into fun shaped mold. You can add colors to your soap as well.

Magickal Headspace Shower

Now that you have your magickal ritual soap, it's time to put it to use. Here are the directions for a very simple way to change your vibrations in 20 minutes or less. Turn on some good music, light a little incense, do whatever feels right to help set the space.

Start by getting 2 glasses of water and placing them on each side of the door going into your bathroom. When you leave this space, you will do so walking through 2 pillars that represent purity of energy/entrance to magickal and/or spiritual realms. You will be stepping through the glasses of water as your magickal self.

Take a nice long slow shower. Don't rush. Become aware of the water and soap on your skin. Clear your mind of mundane thoughts and start to think of how you are going to be spending your sacred or magickal time.

This is also a good time to count your blessings, to think of all the things that you are blessed to be thankful for. Regardless of what you were doing for the evening, you want to enter sacred space from a place of gratitude.

When finished, towel off and take a moment to ground or say a small verse/prayer aloud. Next, purposefully walk through the glasses of water you placed on each side of door knowing you are connected to Higher realms. And now get dressed in that special robe, dress, necklace and of course, cloak and go forth; be Witchy, be magickal, be successful.

In the Fall, I like to

_____

_____

_____

_____

In the Spring, I like to

_____

_____

_____

_____

In the Winter, I like to

_____

_____

_____

_____

In the Summer, I like to

_____

_____

_____

_____

Standing on a mountain top, I see

_____

_____

_____

_____

Walking through the woods make me feel

_____

_____

A mentor is not perfect because

_____

_____

_____

Saying sorry is something I do

_____

_____

_____

The perfect circle cast is

_____

_____

_____

Legacy means to me

_____

_____

_____

I am most afraid when

_____

_____

_____

5 DIVINITY & SPIRIT REALMS

Divinity
Divinity is everything. Everything is Divine.

Within the Many there is One.
For some magickal folks, this is the basis of their relationship with Divinity. They see all the Gods and Goddesses as creating the One.

Within the One there is Many
Now for others, it is the One that creates all the Gods and Goddesses. They see the One as the source of everything.

These are deep topics that we each must answer for ourselves. You must explore and decide for yourself how Divinity connects with/to you. Our Tradition encourages personal experiences/relationships with Divinity.

What representation(s) of Divinity you put on your altar is yours alone to discover.

Different aspects/energies of Divinity will be revealed to us at different seasons in our lives. A fancy way of saying "you will see many faces of the Goddess/God in your lifetime." Sometimes it for a reason, other times it is for a season.

Don't sweat it, Divinity has a sense of humor too, and knows you are new to this path.

As long as you are striving and trying to connect, you will be just fine.

Honor Reverence Respect

The Goddess
She is everything, everywhere.
She is the beautiful Lady of long ago and today.

The God
He is everything, everywhere.
He is the handsome Lord of long ago and today.

Within our Tradition, we use the term "Divinity" to show honor and reverence to all folk's personal relationships with their aspects (Gods & Goddesses). All forms are sacred, and to be respected.

Sabbat's Representations of Divinity
Seasonal representations of Divinity help link us to the land and nature during a Sabbat. There are some really good lore stories available in books and online.

Demeter's daughter, Persephone, is linked to springtime. After being forced to stay in the Underworld with Hades for 6 months, she emerges, bringing spring with her. From this simple lore, we can create a play, a more in-depth story, or even a dance. Be imaginative and be in the season.

Esbat's Representations of Divinity
This time of moon magick is for connecting with all the possibilities that the universe has to offer. Wisely invite a God or Goddess, or none at all. Instead, consider calling a spirit guide(s), elementals, etc. to aide you in the evening's magick.

The cycle of Nature is the key to the Web of Life. Through this the power of the Divine flows. This is where the magick is. Keep your life in tune with nature, and magick will surround you. Honor every full moon and celebrate the Sabbats.

Each relationship with Divinity is unique and personal.

How you venerate Divinity is an individual experience.

Life isn't about finding yourself.
Life is about Creating yourself.
George Bernard Shaw

Connecting to the Land and Ancestral Realms

Find the oldest graveyard/cemetery in local area. Bring a small token, or gift, maybe 3 shiny pennies--what you feel compelled to take with you. Place the tokens at the entrance to the graveyard or upon a grave. Again, you must do what feels right for that place, and the Spirits/energies there.

Find oldest grave in the cemetery. Say a few words, or a small prayer and take a very small handful of dirt from foot of grave, if you are given permission. Again, you will feel it.

When leaving the graveyard don't look back. Often time, magickal folk will turn 3 circles counterclockwise upon exiting the area. This stops any negative energies from attaching or following them. And a pinch of salt thrown over your shoulder while leaving is another common prevention.

Next full moon, place dirt in small dish on your altar. Speak words of honor and remembrance. Afterwards, sprinkle it in your outdoor sacred space, or store in a dark colored glass jar/container to be used for ancestral related workings.

Gather ye Witches, young and old,
Who come to seek mysteries untold.
The Goddess's voice is easy to hear,
Under a full moon loud and clear.
Her Charge is given to Her Priest/ess this eve,
Who know to look within to receive.

My personal prayer to Divinity is

_____

_____

_____

_____

_____

In the East is Air, a place I find

_____

_____

_____

_____

In the South is Fire, a place I find

_____

_____

_____

_____

In the West is Water, a place I find

_____

_____

_____

_____

In the North is Earth, a place I find

_____

_____

_____

_____

For me, Divinity is

_____

_____

_____

_____

When I light a candle to Divinity, I feel

_____

_____

_____

_____

Real magick is

_____

_____

_____

_____

Music in sacred space is

_____

_____

_____

_____

I feel closest to Divinity when I

_____

_____

_____

_____

Honor, reverence, respect means

_____

_____

_____

To connect to Divinity, I will

_____

_____

_____

My strength is

_____

_____

_____

A Saint is

_____

_____

_____

Death is transformation because

_____

_____

_____

_____

6 MAGICKAL TOOLS

Acquiring Magickal Tools

Athame, chalice, incense burner, brass bowl, wand, cauldron, besom, cloak, staff, cane, bottle, candle stick, and the list could go on and on.

Witchery Motto:
Use what you have, use what you need.

Yes, it is nice to have the props, but you really don't need them. Positive attitude, belief, and faith are the cornerstones of success in all magickal endeavors. Now with all that said, physical items help us to have a positive attitude, belief, and faith, so find your balance of what items to put in your magickal cupboard and use.

If you desire a wand, then start asking for one when in magickal space. And don't forget you may need to ask 3-5-7 times, be patient. The Universe will put the perfect one just around the corner for you. Positive attitude, belief and faith will make it happen.

Many magickal folks like looking in thrift stores, flea markets, and garage sales for that perfect item that has journeyed so far to be there in that moment for them. The energies of the item add to the magick that is being created. You will see Witches picking up items and "feeling" them by just taking a few deep breaths and opening up to the energy of the item. Right energy goes in the magick cupboard, wrong energy goes back on the store shelf.

Whether new, used, found, bought or given, once the item is in your care, treat it with respect.

Bless it by washing with moon water, dressing with oils, or smudging.
Store it carefully, and always say kind words when putting back.
Whether you let others touch or use the item is a personal choice.

Anointing (Preparing) A Magickal Item
Used to cleanse/clear an item being used for magickal/sacred purpose.
For every Witch there is a way, and different items may require different energies/methods.

Wash/rinse with Moon water/Holy Water. Place on altar during full moon from dawn to dusk.
Cleanse using elements.
Smudge with sage, herbs and/or tobacco smoke. Hold item-say heartfelt words.

Ultimately you are preparing an item to be used magickally/spiritually. Envision empowerment, blessings, protection.

Consecrating (Blessing) A Magickal Item
To dedicate a person, place or item to a/for Divine purpose. (to give a purpose to)

Ways to consecrate:
Heartfelt words.
Full, new, dark moon ritual for purpose.
Sigils, signs, runes carved or marked upon item. Herbs & oils blended for purpose.

You will anoint and then consecrate many items: crystals, stones, items used in workings, wands, grimoires, items that you use magickally/spiritually. Take the time to develop Your Way in this process.

Have a quick and simple "on the go Witchy way" and a special more depth method for those magickal items that need a more intricate process.

On the Go Witchy Way to Anoint/Consecrate/Bless

Here is an example of one way for the "on the go Witchy way" to anoint and then consecrate a magickal item. The other way is you do what "feels right" and makes sense to you.

Hold item in your hand. Pick one (1) of the following:
-pour blessed water on item
-say heartfelt words
-place one (1) drop of blessed oil blend/essential oil of choice in palm of left hand and rub on item
-smudge with sage/herbs/tobacco
Say aloud "This (item) is free of all negativity and blessed. Within me is the power. Selah."

Example of special more depth method for anointing/blessing/consecrating Refer to Three Books of Occult Philosophy by Cornelia Agrippa or create your own.

Blessed Book/Journal/B.O.S./Grimoire

There is no one perfect magickal personal journal that works for every Witch. Some call it a book or grimoire, others a journal, and still other Witches call theirs a Book of Shadows or Bos.

It is your book, name it, own it. Find a blank book/3 ring binder/scraps of paper taped together and call it yours. Once you have found your perfect magickal journal, start treating it as a magickal tool. Be respectful and take care of it.

On the first page write a book blessing/protection on it by hand. Write anything else you feel compelled to. Take your book and lay on the altar during the next full moon, open to the blessing and read aloud. Let lay open upon the altar while in sacred space if doing other magick.

When leave circle, take the book with you.

Some Witches have only one (1) bos while others have several-one for spells, one for herbs, one for journaling. Also, Witches may acquire a new/different bos when starting a new season/journey, subject matter, or because it felt right.

Cite Sources
Citing sources helps to keep our history alive. Modern magickal folks have some great talent to draw upon. Doreen Valiente's Charge of the Goddess, Raymond Buckland's works, Michael Howard's prose and a host of other inspired writers that have made their works available to us all. Just as you would want credit for your work, give them their due.

Be proud of your research. Simply writing sources at the bottom of any ritual or spell with a date is all that is needed. That way in 20 years from now you will know the 'when & where' of it. Believe me when I say that those notes from 20 years ago are needed, because after several years, memories will fade.

If I cannot remember what I had for dinner two nights ago, I will never remember who wrote what part of the Imbolc ritual 17 years ago. It is really best to write it down. Also, make sure to write your name at bottom of any original rituals or workings (spells) that you may do.

Awaken.
You are not here by accident.
You are the awakening that breathes the
magick of love and light into a troubled world.
You will be tested and checked on your path.
You will prove to be the survivor you have
always been.
Rise, release the past, and be the hope of
humanity that you truly are.
You are the highest vibration.

I use Blessed Moon Water for

_____

_____

_____

_____

When I stand under a Full Moon, I feel

_____

_____

_____

_____

When I stand under a New Moon, I feel

_____

_____

_____

_____

If I could make a megalith structure, it would be

My favorite empowerment mantra is

I like being Witchy because

On a cold frosty night, I like to

My magickal journal is

When I work magick, I like to

Three magickal ingredients for blessings would be

Three magickal ingredients for protection would be

Life is what we choose, I choose

The voice of Divinity inside me is

When I feel uneasy about a situation, I do

7 MAGICKAL TIDBITS

Crystal Charging
Anoint and consecrate crystals using a method that resonates with you, or one of the ways previously stated. Lay crystals on altar under a waxing full moon or during the time of the new moon.

If possible, you want to leave them on the altar from dawn to dusk. Leave crystals on altar 2-3 hours min. if not able to.

Kitchen Witchery Basics
Always stir clockwise
Energize food with good thoughts
Do all preparations in a loving spirit
Be mindful and grateful
Home and hearth are sacred

Manifestation Box
Also called a creation box, wish box, or intention box. This can be a powerful for creating the life you want. Place things (items representing or petitions) in the box that you want to attract or manifest in your life.

Each time you do, your sending an affirmation to the universe, and your intentions will begin to draw your desires.

Attracting Prosperity

Wash down your front door with blessed water and a little essential oil of mint to refresh the vibrations and welcome in luck, wealth, and abundance. Peppermint, spearmint, or mint, all work well. Witchy Wise- put mixture in a spray bottle and use liberally on your front door.

Ward off Negative/Dark Energies

If you feel influenced by negative energies, light a black candle in front of a mirror and say:

Any darker evil force may now return unto its source.
May my home and I be free,
safe and well.
So mote it be.
Blessed Be.

Magickal All-purpose Substitutions

White candles can be substituted for any color candle.
Quartz can be substituted for any type of crystal.
Rosemary can be substituted for any type of herb.
Tobacco can be substituted for any poisonous herb.
Rose can be substituted for any flower.

Magickal Days of the Week

Monday-Moon-White
Purity, spirituality, cleansing, psychic endeavors, healing, dream works

Tuesday-Mars-Red
Manifesting physical energies, passion, strength, ambition, protection, confidence, masculine goals

Wednesday-Mercury-Violet
Travel/change,career/job, research, knowledge, planning magickal work, writing

Thursday-Jupiter-Blue
Luck, legal matters, spiritual celebrations, business

Friday-Venus-Pink
Feminine energies, fertility, relationships, healing, peace, artistic abilities

Saturday-Saturn-Black
Bindings, endings, loss, renewal, transformations, home issues

Sunday-Sun-Yellow
Success, problem solving, friendship, healing, personal empowerment, illuminations

Basic Colors for Candle Magick
White- spirituality, peace, higher self, purity
Black-banishing against negativity, protection, binding
Brown-home protection, animals, stability, family, material goods
Red-vital energy, strength, passion, courage, fast action, last charisma
Pink-romantic love, emotional healing, friendship, caring, nurturing, self-love
Orange-business, success, justice, opportunity, celebration, ambition
Yellow-intelligence, learning, focus, memory, joy, comfort, hope
Green-nature, physical healing, money, abundance, fertility, growth
Blue-communication, traveling, inspiration, calm, creativity, forgiveness
Purple-influence psychic abilities, wisdom, authority, hidden knowledge
Silver-intuition, psychism, dreams, femininity, the moon
Gold-wealth, luck, prosperity, money making, happiness, the sun

To Be Pagan
"When one defines oneself as Pagan, it means he or
she follows an earth or nature religion.
One that sees the Divine manifest in all creations.
The cycles of nature are our holy days.
The earth is our temple.
It's plants and creatures are partners and teachers.
We worship a Deity that is both male and female.
A mother Goddess and a father God, who together
created all that is, was, or will be.
We respect life, cherish the free will of sentient
beings, and accept the sacredness of all creation."

Edain McCoy

My perfect Witchy day would be

_____

_____

_____

_____

Mother Nature reminds me

_____

_____

_____

_____

My favorite Full Moon incense is

_____

_____

_____

My favorite New Moon incense is

_____

_____

_____

The perfect time to sit on the beach is

_____

_____

_____

Shadow working is something I

_____

_____

_____

I would have a magickal garden full of

_____

_____

_____

My favorite time for spell casting is

_____

_____

_____

On rainy days, I want to

_____

_____

_____

_____

My doubts are

_____

_____

_____

_____

The Light means

_____

_____

_____

_____

The Dark means

_____

_____

_____

_____

My best assets are

_____

_____

_____

_____

Faith is

_____

_____

_____

_____

I need to learn to accept

_____

_____

8 RITES & WORKINGS

The Perfect Ritual
Is the one that happens in the moment. When you are doing what
feels right. When everyone involved connects with whatever energy
is being created.

Long texts of ancient script and a theatrical altar with cool music in
the background is not going to connect folks any deeper than
standing in their own backyard if the correct energy is not there.

The most tingly energy charged rituals always seems to be the
simple ones with folks you are already connected to magickally.

Simple invocations with words vibrated and a common goal is a very
good start for an awesome experience.

Remember magick take many forms. From spoken words, to candle
burning, to mixing oils, to something as simple as posting an image
on the wall; pure energy, focus and intent are what transforms
simple actions, words, and gestures into magick.

As you read each line and spell,
learn one lesson very well.
It's not the words or chants you do.
It's not the tools that see you through.
They simply help you work your plan,
The power is in your hand.
Words and deeds may play a part,
But true magick lies within the heart.

Rite of Beginning/Dedication

For many of folks, this is the most important ritual that they will ever do. It is a magickal birth date. Things will be counted from that day forward. It will become a treasured memory; a marker in our life's journey.

Best to keep it simple, well-said, and heartfelt. Don't try to make a big production of this moment. Let the universe decorate. It is about keeping it real.

With salt I consecrate and bless this circle.
In the Divine name of the Goddess
and the horned God.
Blessed be.

I invoke and call upon thee,
Oh Mother Goddess, creatress of life
and soul of the infinite universe.
By candle flame and incense smoke,
I do invoke thee to bless this rite,
and to grant me admittance
to the company of thy loving children.
O beautiful Goddess of life and rebirth,
known as Cerridwen, Astarte, Athena, Bridget,
Diana, Isis, Hecate, Inanna, Aphrodite, Aradia,

and by many other Divine names.

In this consecrated circle of candlelight,
I do pledge myself to honor thee,
to love thee,
to serve thee well, for as long as I shall live.
I promised to respect, and obey the law
of love unto all living things.
I promised to never reveal craft secrets
to any man or woman not of the same path.
I swear I shall strive to harm none.
O Goddess Queen of all Witches,
I do open my heart and soul to thee.
So mote it be.

I invoke and call upon thee,
O great horned God of Pagans,
Lord of all green woodlands,
and Father of all things wild and free.

By candle flame and incense smoke,
do I invoke thee to bless this rite.
O Great Horned God of Death,
and all that comes after,
who was known as Cerunnos, Ra, Apollo, Neptune, Vulcan, Hercules,
Pan, Daghda, Odin, and by many other Divine names.

In this consecrated circle of candlelight,
I do pledge myself to honor thee,
to love thee,
to serve thee well, for as long as I shall live.

O Great Horned God of Peace and Love,
I do open my heart and soul to thee.
So mote it be.

5 Witchy Ways to Cast a Magickal Circle

There are many, many ways to cast a circle and create magickal space. The object is to create a safe and protected area for either celebrating or working magick in.

For every Witch, there is their own personal creative way to connect with a space. There is no one way, right way or only way; just the way that works for you.

Indoors- clean, cleared, uncluttered
Outdoors-calm, quiet, safe

Fill the space with your presence/energy. This is the beginning of the in-between. In a time that has no time, a place where day/night, joy/sorrow, death/rebirth meet as one. This is where the magick is.

These casts can all be used individually, combined, or twisted in whatever way you are compelled to do. Don't be afraid to try a different circle cast and see which one resonates with your personal Witchy magick.

1. Walk a circle three times and speak in rhyme

This can be a short 3 or 4 line prose, or long verses. This is probably the most common or well-known way to cast a magickal circle among modern Witches. Take the time to not only memorize the words but to "know" the words. Being able to put all your energy in each word said will create a powerful sacred circle.

2. Smudge with Sage/Sweetgrass/Tobacco

Make sure to swirl smoke throughout the entire area. This method has been used in many cultures, and civilizations. Its' origins are lost in the mists of time. Take your time with this one. Break up the area into quarters, and really concentrate on each space before moving to the next quarter.

3. Salt and/or herbs

Spread salt/herbs in area working or create a circle. Use salt alone, or blend with dirt, herbs and/or spices. There are many wonderful natural salts available to us today very inexpensively found. Pink, black, rock, Himalayan, and Celtic sea salt are just a few types of salt to name. With herbs, use what is locally grown or resonates with you. There are literally hundreds to choose from.

Mixture used at the Cottage is a natural fine salt blended with ash from a sacred bonfire, red brick dust, and a dash of black pepper. Again, this is your magickal recipe to create.

4. Spiral in and out

Simply walk a spiral inward toward your working area or altar. Words or silence (what feels right), ground with each step taken. When finished, spiral outwards until you feel a return to mundane space and time. Often, you will actually feel the temperature change when you have returned to mundane space and time.

5. Dance and drum

When the moon is full and bright in the night sky, and you have a group of Witchery folks circling a sacred fire (bonfire), there is no better way than to dance, Witches dance. The energy that will be created is Amazing with a capitol "A". If you don't have drums, consider playing some cool Witchy tunes.
Cast the circle of your Spirit. Do what feels right.

"Slowly toward the sacred Light, spiral in.
Walk around, walk around, walk around.
This is the Witch's realm.
Softly leave the in-between, spiral out.
Walk around, walk around, walk around.
This was a Witch's dream."

Witches' Cottage Circle Cast

All members are required to memorize the Witches' Cottage circle
cast.

Black spirits and white,
Red spirits and grey,
Harken to the rune I say.
Four points of the circle weave our spell,
East, South, West, North, our tale to tell.
East is for the break of day,
South is for the noontide hour.
In the West is twilight grey,
And in the North is black for the place of power.
Three times round the circle is cast,
Great Ones and Witches of the past,
Witness it and guard it fast.
As above, so below.
We are now in a time that has no time. A place that has no place. We
are in the between.
So mote it be.
Blessed Be.   from original by Doreen Valiente

Book Blessing

Hand write your name/sigil on top of page of first page, and then
write down the protection/blessing; either the one in this book or
your personal one.

During the time of the full moon, take your book outside. Stand so
the light of the moon falls upon the words in your book. Slowly and
with deep intent, speak the words aloud, binding them to the book.

If you have an altar set up, lay book upon it for a couple of hours. Let
it soak up all that full moon energy.

Record in your book the date this is done.

Make sure you are in the right headspace to do this activity. Be
happy with each word written down, have no distractions, play good
music, drink a glass of wine.

Spend an evening with your new bos, planning and dreaming of all
the magickal possibilities to be written down in it. Touch it, hold it,
stroke it, or stare at it from across the room. Tell it how truly special
it is to you. This is your magickal grimoire that in time will tell its'
own stories. Celebrate this moment.

The following book blessing was written in 2002 by Taren S, for all
members to use, modify, or be inspired to write their own personal
book blessing.

Words of Wisdom this book shall be.
Acts of Honor recorded in thee.
Herbs, spells and lore,
From the heart like the Ancients before.
Knowing that the Mystery is within,
These pages have but words to lend.
Remember Karmic Law has three,
Wisdom and Honor are the key.
Protected by elemental forces that be,
Forever safe, never for the cowan to see.
This book of mine, I give to the Divine.
So mote it be.
Blessed Be.

Moon Blessed Water Working

This is Witchy Holy Water. It can be used in spell work, cooking,
blessings, and anything else you can think of.

Here is a chance to be very imaginative in spell crafting. Sprinkle on
walkways and across doorways to attract positive energies or deter
negative ones. Add when mopping floors. Use daily in meals, teas,
and baths.

In addition to making a full moon blessed water, you can also use the various types of moon energies to influence the properties of the water. Basically, you are making a moon flavored water. Use it in spell work according to its properties.

Flavored Moon Waters

Waning	Full	Waxing
-sending away	-blessing	-bringing forth
-making smaller	-creating	-making bigger

Super- intensifies water's energies
New- beginnings, new possibilities
Dark- wisdom of self, speaking with spirits, curses, attracting demons, create envy-hate-greed-jealousy
Blood-add strength, neutral
Blue-extra special blessings

IMPORTANT!

Charged moon water is only good until next moon cycle. The energies change at that time. Moon water is in the present and should be used as such.

Use spring water that has moved naturally and not gone through metal pipes, and a glass container/jar that the moonlight can be seen through.

Or buy spring water and run it through a filter twice and use an empty plastic lemonade jug (if clumsy, this is the way to go).

Be creative. We are magickal folks, and creating is what we do best.

By the blessings of the Ancient Ones. *hold container into the
moonlight
For the good of all with harm to none.
In all times and every space.
Let the power flow   **pour small amount towards East
Let the power flow   **pour small amount towards South
Let the power flow   **pour small amount towards West
Let the power flow   **pour small amount towards North

As from the beginning, the Power has risen and calls to us.
In the wax and wane of the cycle, when sacred fires are lit, we
Witches are smiled upon.
The gathering of forces in moon's water is the gift we are given.
To be used wisely for healing, reverence and a wise mage's work.
As the water shall pour, the power will flow.
Touched by the Gods and Elementals,   **pass among
Embodied with the good of the universe.   folks in circle
Charged by all who stand in this circle. Sacred water this shall be.

**all repeat aloud rest
I conjure thee three times three.
As it is said, so shall it be done.
For the good of all, with harm to none.
This formula is done.   **place containers on altar
Mote it be.
Blessed be.

Leave moon water containers on altar after ritual and let folks gather
when going home.

Craft Night!

Decorate moon water containers with ribbons, magickal symbols
and other nifty things you can think of.
Makes it easier to identify each other's containers and it is an
evening of fun and cocktails.

Besom (broom) Blessing

All brooms (new/old) are blessed yearly. Make or buy a broom with natural materials. Decorate or leave plain. This magickal tool is an expression/extension of you. Traditional time to bless is February's full moon with a bonfire & dancing.

This working is an excellent example of use of sacred power numbers 3 x (times) 3. Dance around bonfire (real or pretend) with your besom and loudly chant the following:

Witches of the past, who have kept the hearthstone,
Hear my call, hear my call, hear my call.
I claim my right and ask for blessings tonight.
Hear my call, hear my call, hear my call.
Filled with magick, this broom shall be.
Hear my call, hear my call, hear my call.
A sacred tool, from past to present.
Bless this broom, bless this broom, bless this broom.
In dark and light, it will never fail.
Bless this broom, bless this broom, bless this broom.
The power of the universe is wrapped within.
Bless this broom, bless this broom, bless this broom.
This broom of mine, I give to the Divine.
So mote it be. Blessed be.   11/97 Taren S

Initiation Into The Tradition, Outdoor Version

A member of the Coven, the Challenger, should step onto the path in front of initiate. They might want to wear a mask. They take the sword that they carry and say: *"Who comes to the Crossroads?"*
The initiate answers: *"It is I, (Craft name), child of earth and starry heaven."*
The Challenger holds the point of the sword up to the initiate's heart, and says:
"You are about to enter a vortex of power, a place beyond imagining, where birth and death, dark and light, joy and pain, meet and make one. You are about to step between the worlds, beyond time, outside the realm of your human life. For know, it is better to fall on my

blade and perish than to make the attempt with fear in thy heart!"
The initiate answers: *"I tread this path of my own free will."*
The Challenger replies: *"Prepare for death and rebirth."*
The Challenger grounds their sword to the Earth.
The Crone now leads the initiate to each of the four corners and introduces them to the Guardians, going deosil.

"Hail Guardians and Ancestors of the East and all the Mighty Ones of all things magickal. Behold _____ (new name), who will now be made Priestess and Witch."

The initiate is brought back to the altar.
The Crone says:
"Blessed be thy feet, that have brought thee in these ways.
Blessed be thy knees, that shall kneel at the sacred altar.
Blessed be thy womb, without which we would not be.
Blessed be thy breasts, formed in beauty.
Blessed be thy lips, that shall utter the Sacred Names."

The Crone asks the initiate:
"Are you willing to swear the oath?" (I am)
Who asks to be part of the magick of this circle? (Name)
Why do you come? (I am returning home.)
How do you come? (With an open heart.)
Welcome home. You have returned to the magick of your spirit.
From this day forward, step into the world with this knowledge.
(give Initiate the black hunting hat of our Tradition)
Light the eternal flame that your spirit knows. ** initiate lights white Divinity candle.
Pour blessed waters upon your feet to protect your steps. **initiate sprinkles moon water on feet.
Let sweet incense surround you. **folks present wave lit incense/sage bundle around person.
Put your name to the earth. **initiate writes magickal name/sigil in the dirt.
Do you pledge to protect the names of Witches who now call you

sister/brother? (Yes)
Do you pledge to always strive to bring Honor and Wisdom into our
magickal and sacred spaces? (Yes)
Do you pledge to keep silent of what you shall learn? (Yes)

Initiate kneels before altar and reads aloud-
"This is the Charge of the Coven:
That I will keep secret what I am asked to keep secret, and never
divulge the names or dwelling places of our people unless by their
consent.
That I will learn and try to master the Art Magickal; but ever
remember the rune: "What good be the tools without the inner light?
What good be the magick without wisdom and sight?"
That in due course I will strive to find a worthy pupil in magick, to
whom in future years I can hand down the knowledge I acquire.
That I will never use the Art Magickal merely to impress foolish
persons, nor for any wrongful end.
That I will help the Craft of the Wise, and hold its honor as I would
my own.
Know that none can escape the fate, be it curse or blessing, which
they make for themselves, either in this life or in another life."

The Crone says: *"Repeat after me:*
'I, _____, do of my own free will most solemnly swear to protect,
help and defend my sisters and brothers of the Art and to keep the
Coven's Charge.
I always keep secret all that must not be revealed.
This do I swear on my mother's womb and my hopes of future lives,
mindful that my measure has been taken, and in the presence of the
Mighty Ones.'
All between my two hands belongs to the Goddess."
The initiate repeats the oath.

The Coven shouts: *"So mote it be!"*
The Crone says: *"Arise and be anointed."*

The Crone then makes an X mark on the initiate's forehead, breast and genitals while saying:

"May your mind be free. May your heart be free. May your body be free.
Only Higher realms and yourself, will hold you accountable to the vows you have taken.
May the path rise to meet you with the best possible lessons and experiences in all Realms.
Guardians, Ancestors, and Spirits of Old, witness this Witch's return to the magickal circles of her/his spirit.
Protect and guide this magickal journey. Welcome Home, Witch."

Read Charge of Goddess or whatever else initiate may desire. Now all should dance upon the dirt and give blessings to the person. Use drums or CD music. We once used Loreena McKennitt's Mummer's Dance. It was very powerful.

The service goes on as usual, be it New or Full Moon or Sabbat. Before the Circle is opened, the new initiate is taken to the four corners again and introduced to the Guardians again.

Inspired from: Starhawk; "The Spiral Dance: Rebirth of the Ancient Religion of the Goddess"; HarperRow 1979
Valiente, Doreen; "Witchcraft for Tomorrow"; Phoenix Publishing 1985

Within every person drawn to the path of witchcraft
resides the powerful spirit of a witch.
In order to find yourself, and your path,
you must first push aside what the world has taught
you.

A field of red poppies makes me want to

_____

_____

_____

_____

My favorite season is

_____

_____

_____

_____

The sound of the ocean waves is

_____

_____

_____

_____

Spell crafting in rhyme is something I

_____

_____

_____

_____

When I do a house cleansing, I like to

_____

_____

_____

_____

When I do a house blessing, I like to

_____

_____

If I could have any animal has a familiar, it would be

_____

_____

_____

On my altar right now is

_____

_____

_____

I am most proud of myself when

_____

_____

_____

My 1 year Witchy goal is

_____

_____

_____

My 5 year Witchy goal is

_____

_____

_____

To "take the high road" means

_____

_____

_____

My truth is

_____

_____

_____

The worst thing I can do is

_____

_____

_____

It is okay not to like someone because

_____

_____

_____

My perfect wand would be

_____

_____

_____

When I cast a circle, I

_____

_____

9 THE WAY

Our Guiding Tenets

We have an incredible array of knowledge in this day and age. There was a time not too long ago when this was not so. For many covens, a little knowledge became a treasured secret. This is what happened to "The Witch's Way".

Written by Ed Fitch and passed unpublished among covens and groups in the 1970's, it became part of the foundation of many magickal Traditions in America. Sometime around 1978, our Tradition embraced these wise words. We encourage all Witchy folks to listen to the wisdom of the Great Mother as said through Ed.

While written in middle English with a lot of Thou's, Thereofs, Thus, and sometimes all together confusing, it is still an amazing modern document that should be included in our grimoires.

When I was first read the Witch's Way in the early 1980's, it inspired me to be so much more than what I knew to be possible at the time. I wrote it down in my personal journal to keep close to my heart. Over the years whenever I am feeling a little lost, I have sat and read the words again, always finding comfort and wisdom.

Modified from the original "The Pagan Way" by Ed Fitch, with his permission and encouragement.

The Witch's Way
1. Chivalry is a high code of honor which is of most ancient Pagan origin and must be lived by all who follow the Old Ways.
2. It must be kenned that thoughts and intent put forth on this Middle-Earth will wax strong in other worlds beyond, and return...bringing into creation, on this world, that which had been sent forth. Thus, one should exercise discipline, for "as ye do plant, so shall ye harvest."
3. It is only by preparing our minds to be as Gods that we can ultimately attain godhead.
4. "This above all......to thine own self be true..."
5. A Witch's word must have the validity of a signed and witnessed oath. Thus, give thy word sparingly, but adhere to it like iron.
6. Refrain from speaking ill of others, for not all truths of the matter may be known.
7. Pass not unverified words about another, for hearsay is, in large part, a thing of falsehoods.
8. Be thou honest with others and have them known that honesty is likewise expected of them.
9. The fury of the moment plays folly with the truth; to keep one's head is a virtue.
10. Contemplate always the consequences of thine acts upon others. Strive not to harm.
11. Diverse covens may well have diverse views on love between members and with others. When a coven, clan, or grove is visited or joined, one should discern quietly their practices, and abide thereby.
12. Dignity, a gracious manner, and a good humor are much to be admired.
13. As a Witch, thou hast power, and thy powers wax strongly as wisdom increases. Therefore, exercise discretion in the use thereof.
14. Courage and honor endure forever. Their echoes remain when the mountains have crumbled to dust.

15. Pledge friendship and fealty to those who so warrant. Strengthen others of the Brethren and they shall strengthen thee.

16. Thou shalt not reveal the secrets of another Witch or Coven. Others have labored long and hard for them, and cherish them as treasures.

17. Though there may be differences between those of the Old Ways, those who are once-born must see nothing, and must hear nothing.

18. Those who follow the mysteries should be above reproach in the eyes of the world.

19. The laws of the land should be obeyed whenever possible and within reason, for in the main they have been chosen with wisdom.

20. Have pride in thyself, and seek perfection in body and in mind. For the Lay has said, "How canst thou honor another unless thou give honor to thyself first".

21.Those who seek the Mysteries should consider themselves as select of the Gods, for it is they who lead the race of humankind to the highest thrones and beyond the very stars.

In the shadows we do stand,
We are the hope of the land.
The Universe is in our keep,
Her mysteries are ours seek.
Live your life in the here and now,
Remembering, honor is a Witch's vow.

ABOUT THE AUTHOR

Taren S stood in her first magickal circle at 17 yrs. old in the backwoods of North Carolina with a coven of Southern conjuring Witches. Their magickal roots are traced over 100 years in the region. She was initiated as a High Priestess within the American Witchcraft Tradition in 1995. Along the East Coast, she has stood as HPS at many large festivals and gatherings. Her original coven has hived off several times since forming over 25 years ago.

For over a decade, she worked at a Haitian Voodoo Priest's botanica (magick shop) as a spiritual counselor and professional tarot card reader in the Lowcountry of South Carolina. Furthering her magickal and spiritual path, she was initiated as a Mama Bridget within American-Haitian Voodoo.

Currently, she lives in San Diego county and is the founder of The House of Witchcraft. You can find out more information at houseofwitchcraft.com.

"I don't have to understand your magick, I just need to respect that you are doing magick"
Taren S

Made in the USA
Middletown, DE
27 September 2023

39550580R00050